EXPLORING THE STATES

Maryland

THE OLD LINE STATE

by Patrick Perish

BLASTOFF! READERS
5

BELLWETHER MEDIA · MINNEAPOLIS, MN

Note to Librarians, Teachers, and Parents:

Blastoff! Readers are carefully developed by literacy experts and combine standards-based content with developmentally appropriate text.

Level 1 provides the most support through repetition of high-frequency words, light text, predictable sentence patterns, and strong visual support.

Level 2 offers early readers a bit more challenge through varied simple sentences, increased text load, and less repetition of high-frequency words.

Level 3 advances early-fluent readers toward fluency through increased text and concept load, less reliance on visuals, longer sentences, and more literary language.

Level 4 builds reading stamina by providing more text per page, increased use of punctuation, greater variation in sentence patterns, and increasingly challenging vocabulary.

Level 5 encourages children to move from "learning to read" to "reading to learn" by providing even more text, varied writing styles, and less familiar topics.

Whichever book is right for your reader, Blastoff! Readers are the perfect books to build confidence and encourage a love of reading that will last a lifetime!

This edition first published in 2014 by Bellwether Media, Inc.

No part of this publication may be reproduced in whole or in part without written permission of the publisher. For information regarding permission, write to Bellwether Media, Inc., Attention: Permissions Department, 5357 Penn Avenue South, Minneapolis, MN 55419.

Library of Congress Cataloging-in-Publication Data

Perish, Patrick.
 Maryland / by Patrick Perish.
   pages cm. – (Blastoff! readers. Exploring the states)
 Includes bibliographical references and index.
 Summary: "Developed by literacy experts for students in grades three through seven, this book introduces young readers to the geography and culture of Maryland"–Provided by publisher.
 ISBN 978-1-62617-019-3 (hardcover : alk. paper)
 1. Maryland–Juvenile literature. I. Title.
 F181.3.P47 2014
 975.2–dc23
                                                                    2013002287

Printed in the United States of America, North Mankato, MN.

Table of Contents

Where Is Maryland?

Hancock

West Virginia

Washington, D.C.

Virginia

Maryland is located in the middle of the East Coast of the United States. It shares a border with Pennsylvania to the north and Delaware to the east. Washington, D.C. and Virginia are its southwestern neighbors. West Virginia lies to the west.

Pennsylvania

fun fact

Maryland is a narrow state. Near the town of Hancock, it is less than 2 miles (3.2 kilometers) wide!

Baltimore

★Annapolis

Chesapeake Bay

Delaware

Maryland

N
W   E
S

Atlantic Ocean

The Chesapeake Bay divides Maryland almost in half. On the western side of the bay sits the capital city, Annapolis. Across the bay is Maryland's Eastern Shore. In the southeast, the coastline stretches 31 miles (50 kilometers) along the Atlantic Ocean.

History

In the 1600s, the King of England gave the Calvert family land in the Americas to start a **colony**. Many **Native** American tribes were already living in the area. In 1767, the Mason-Dixon Line established the border between Maryland and Pennsylvania. Maryland became the seventh state in 1788.

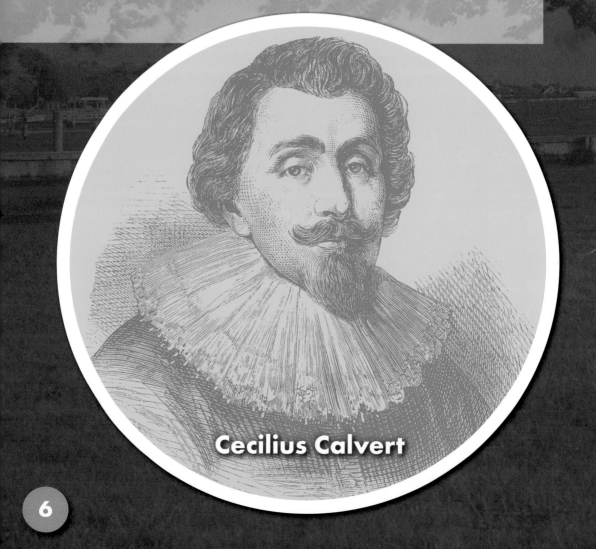

Cecilius Calvert

Maryland Timeline!

1200: Native Americans settle permanent villages in the area.

1608: Captain John Smith explores the Chesapeake Bay.

1632: King Charles I gives land in the Americas to Cecilius Calvert. The land is named Maryland after Queen Henrietta Maria.

1634: British settlers land on Saint Clements Island in the Potomac River. They start the first town in Maryland, called Saint Mary's City.

1814: The British fire on Fort McHenry in Baltimore. Francis Scott Key watches the attack and writes "The Star-Spangled Banner."

1862: The Battle of Antietam is fought near Sharpsburg, Maryland.

1864: Maryland ends slavery within the state.

1952: The Chesapeake Bay Bridge opens. It connects the Eastern and Western Shores.

John Smith

Fort McHenry

Potomac River

The Land

Maryland's Climate
average °F

spring
Low: 44°
High: 65°

summer
Low: 66°
High: 86°

fall
Low: 49°
High: 68°

winter
Low: 28°
High: 45°

Did you know?
Western Maryland has cold winters and hot summers. Eastern Maryland has warmer weather because it is closer to the ocean.

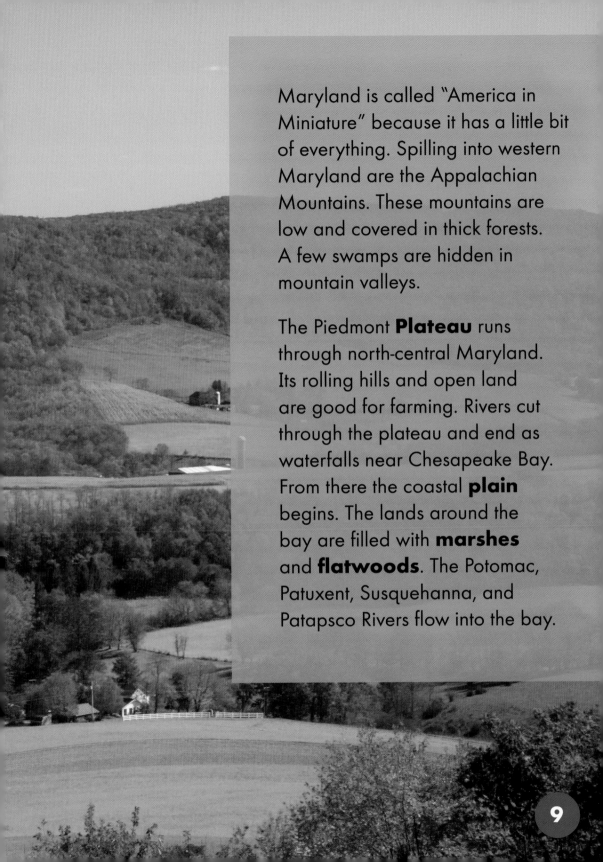

Maryland is called "America in Miniature" because it has a little bit of everything. Spilling into western Maryland are the Appalachian Mountains. These mountains are low and covered in thick forests. A few swamps are hidden in mountain valleys.

The Piedmont **Plateau** runs through north-central Maryland. Its rolling hills and open land are good for farming. Rivers cut through the plateau and end as waterfalls near Chesapeake Bay. From there the coastal **plain** begins. The lands around the bay are filled with **marshes** and **flatwoods**. The Potomac, Patuxent, Susquehanna, and Patapsco Rivers flow into the bay.

The Chesapeake Bay

The Chesapeake Bay splits Maryland down the middle. It is the largest **estuary** in North America. Here, freshwater from the rivers mixes with saltwater from the ocean. This makes the perfect home for shellfish. For years, **watermen** caught blue crabs, oysters, and other shellfish from the bay. They used sailboats called skipjacks.

The bay area is a popular place to live. This causes some problems. New houses mean fewer forests. **Runoff** from nearby farms and cities pollutes the water. Oysters naturally **filter** water, but overfishing has brought down their numbers. Today, communities are working hard to clean up the bay.

fun fact !

In the late 1800s, oysters could filter the entire bay in three to seven days. Now it takes almost a year to filter the same amount of water.

oysters

Wildlife

Maryland's landscapes are home to a great variety of wildlife. The bay waters are perfect for clams, oysters, and other shellfish. Ducks, swans, and other waterbirds love the wetlands. Storks and egrets stalk the shallow waters for tasty fish and crabs. Lucky visitors may spot the **endangered** Puritan tiger beetle hunting along sandy beaches.

On the Eastern Shore, the rare Delmarva fox squirrel lives in the loblolly pine and cypress forests. Black bears and weasels roam the mountains. In spring, spotted salamanders gather to breed in the swamps.

spotted salamander

Delmarva fox squirrel

Puritan tiger beetle

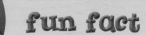 **fun fact**

Assateague Island off Maryland's eastern coast is home to a herd of wild ponies. Stories say the ponies arrived on the island in the 1600s. They had escaped a sinking Spanish ship.

Hooper Strait Lighthouse
Chesapeake Bay Maritime Museum

The Battle of Antietam was fought near Sharpsburg, Maryland. Today, many people visit this **Civil War** battlefield. Another important battle site is **Fort** McHenry in Baltimore. The British attacked it during the **War of 1812**. Francis Scott Key watched the attack from a ship. He was inspired to write the words that later became "The Star-Spangled Banner."

The Chesapeake Bay Maritime Museum is in Saint Michaels, Maryland. It has the largest collection of Chesapeake Bay boats in the world. These include bugeyes, skipjacks, and tugboats. The museum also has a working **boatyard**.

Battle of Antietam

fun fact

Reenactors like to act out the Battle of Antietam. The battle was the bloodiest Civil War fight.

Baltimore

Baltimore is the largest city in Maryland. It is home to around 620,000 people. The city has been an important shipping center since its beginning in 1729. Built in the 1800s, the Baltimore and Ohio Railroad carried goods inland.

Today, Baltimore's Inner Harbor has many unique attractions. The Maryland Science Center features a dinosaur dig. At the National Aquarium, visitors can catch a dolphin show. There are also many historic ships in Baltimore's Inner Harbor. Visitors can explore the USS *Constellation*, an all-sail ship built in 1853!

fun fact

One of the most important American horse races is held in Baltimore. The Preakness Stakes draws huge crowds of people every year.

The Preakness Stakes

watermen

Farming and fishing have always had a central role in Maryland. Today the state has almost 13,000 farms. They raise chickens, dairy cattle, corn, and soybeans. Along the coasts, watermen work to provide the country with fresh seafood.

Many Marylanders work in science and technology. Scientists at NASA's Goddard Space Flight Center are some of the nation's best. They build spacecraft and tools to study the universe. Most people in Maryland have **service jobs**. More than 8 million **tourists** flock to Ocean City every year for its famous **hospitality**. Marylanders work hard to provide beautiful beaches, shops, and restaurants for vacationers.

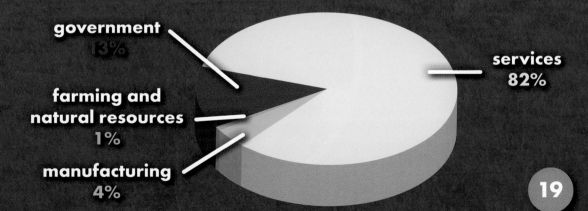

Where People Work in Maryland

government
13%

services
82%

farming and
natural resources
1%

manufacturing
4%

Playing

Marylanders across the state get outdoors during their free time. Hiking and skiing are popular in western Maryland. People in the bay area enjoy fishing, swimming, and sailing. They can also follow in John Smith's footsteps. The famous captain explored the Chesapeake Bay in the 1600s. Water trails map his journey along the coast.

Jousting is the official sport of Maryland. In the **Middle Ages**, jousters tried to knock each other off their horses with poles called lances. Today, jousters try to spear small rings that hang in midair. Summer contests are held all over Maryland.

Jousting

Crab Cakes

Ingredients:

1 pound crabmeat
2 slices white bread,
  without crusts
1 egg, beaten
1 tablespoon mayonnaise
1 teaspoon
  Dijon-style mustard
1 teaspoon
  Worcestershire sauce
1 tablespoon Old Bay seasoning
2 tablespoons butter

Directions:

1. Make sure there are no pieces of shell in the crabmeat.

2. Tear bread into small pieces and put in medium-size bowl with crabmeat. Add egg, mayonnaise, mustard, Worcestershire sauce, and Old Bay seasoning.

3. Gently mix ingredients by hand. Keep the lumps of crabmeat together as much as possible.

4. Form mixture into six patties.

5. Heat butter in a skillet. Fry cakes until a brown crust forms on both sides of the crab cake, about 4 minutes.

Smith Island cake

Shellfish have always been a big part of Maryland **cuisine**. Oysters on the half shell, clam **chowders**, and stewed scallops are all local favorites. Maryland is most famous for its crab cakes made from Chesapeake Bay blue crabs.

Maryland-style chicken is some of the best in America. It is pan-fried and often served with white gravy. The official dessert of Maryland is Smith Island cake. The cake has six to twelve thin layers. Each is topped with rich chocolate fudge. Berger cookies are another popular treat. These vanilla cookies are hand-dipped in fudge at a shop in Baltimore.

Festivals

March 25 is Maryland Day. This marks the day that settlers first landed in Maryland in 1634. Many cities celebrate with activities that teach people about Maryland's history. Performers act out how early settlers and Native Americans once lived.

Every fall, Saint Mary's County holds an oyster **shucking** competition. The winner becomes the U.S. National Oyster Shucking Champion. The festival also features cook-offs, live music, and plenty of seafood.

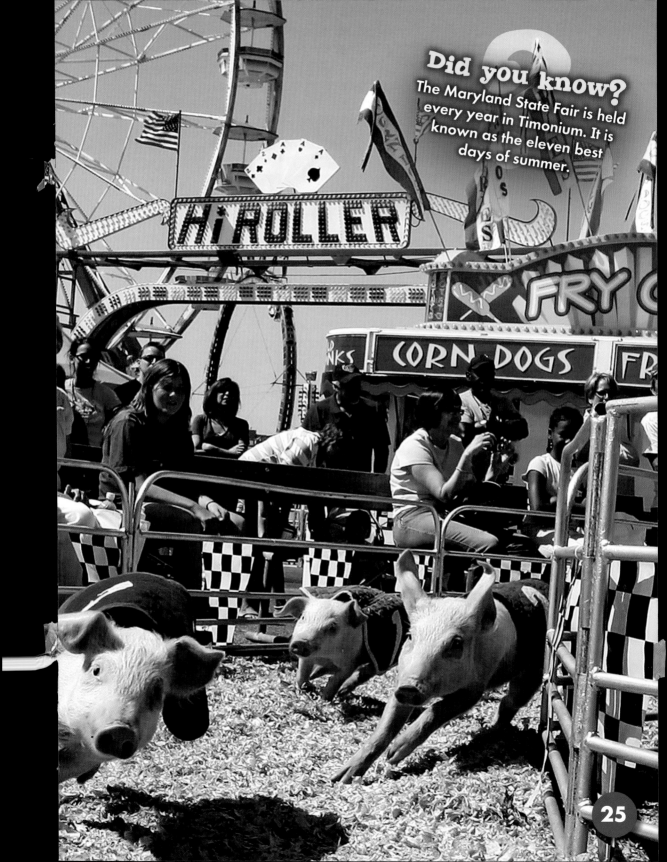

Hi ROLLER

FRY

CORN DOGS

Harriet Tubman and the Underground Railroad

Harriet
Tubman

Harriet Tubman was born into **slavery** in 1820. She lived on a **plantation** in southern Maryland. When she was nearly thirty, she escaped north to freedom. She made it her mission to rescue other enslaved people.

The Underground Railroad was a secret system that helped escaped slaves reach safety. Railroad terms were used as a code. "Stations" were stopping places. "Conductors" hid the slaves and guided them north. Tubman was a conductor on the Underground Railroad for ten years. She led more than 300 people to freedom. Marylanders are proud of their rich history and the progress their state has made.

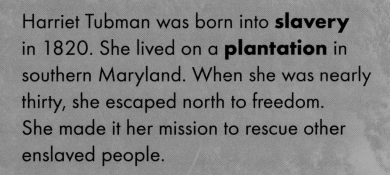

fun fact

Today the Harriet Tubman Underground Railroad Byway offers drivers a glimpse into Tubman's life.

Fast Facts About Maryland

Maryland's Flag

The black and gold flag of the Calvert family has long been used to represent Maryland. The red and white flag of the Crossland family was flown by Confederate Marylanders during the Civil War. The two flags were combined to form the Maryland flag in 1904.

State Flower
black-eyed Susan

State Nicknames:	The Old Line State America in Miniature
State Motto:	*Fatti Maschii, Parole Femine;* "Strong Deeds, Gentle Words"
Year of Statehood:	1788
Capital City:	Annapolis
Other Major Cities:	Baltimore, Columbia, Ocean City
Population:	5,773,552 (2010)
Area:	10,441 square miles (27,042 square kilometers); Maryland is the 42nd largest state.
Major Industries:	services, manufacturing, military, space research
Natural Resources:	farmland, fish, coal
State Government:	141 representatives; 47 senators
Federal Government:	8 representatives; 2 senators
Electoral Votes:	10

State Animal
blue crab

State Bird
Baltimore oriole

Glossary

boatyard—a yard where boats are built, repaired, or stored

chowders—thick, creamy soups made with seafood or vegetables

Civil War—a war between the northern (Union) and southern (Confederate) states that lasted from 1861 to 1865

colony—a territory owned and settled by people from another country

cuisine—a style of cooking unique to a certain area or group of people

endangered—at risk of becoming extinct

estuary—a place where a river meets the ocean

filter—to clean by removing unwanted materials

flatwoods—forests located in low, watery areas

fort—a strong building made to protect lands; forts are often occupied by troops and surrounded by other defenses.

hospitality—welcoming treatment of visitors and guests

marshes—wetlands with grasses and plants

Middle Ages—a time period in Europe lasting from about 500 to 1500 CE

native—originally from a specific place

plain—a large area of flat land

plantation—a large farm that grows coffee, cotton, or other crops; plantations are mainly found in warm climates.

plateau—an area of flat, raised land

runoff—water full of chemicals and other materials that flows from fields and roads into water systems

service jobs—jobs that perform tasks for people or businesses

shucking—removing the outer shell

slavery—a system in which certain people are considered property

tourists—people who travel to visit another place

War of 1812—a war between the United States and Britain that took place from 1812 to 1815

watermen—fishers and crabbers of the Chesapeake Bay

To Learn More

AT THE LIBRARY

Cunningham, Kevin. *The Maryland Colony*. New York, N.Y.: Children's Press, 2012.

Mills, Cliff. *Lord Baltimore*. New York, N.Y.: Chelsea House, 2011.

Shone, Rob and Anita Ganeri. *Harriet Tubman: The Life of an African-American Abolitionist*. New York, N.Y.: Rosen Pub. Group, 2005.

ON THE WEB

Learning more about Maryland is as easy as 1, 2, 3.

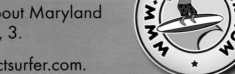

1. Go to www.factsurfer.com.

2. Enter "Maryland" into the search box.

3. Click the "Surf" button and you will see a list of related Web sites.

With factsurfer.com, finding more information is just a click away.

Index

The images in this book are reproduced through the courtesy of: Greg Pease/ Getty Images, front cover; H-D Falkenstein/ ima/ imagebroker.net/ SuperStock, p. 6; Traveler1116, p. 7 (left); Zack Frank, p. 7 (middle); Eurobanks, p. 7 (right); Pat & Chuck Blackley/ Alamy, pp. 8-9; Bill Cobb/ William Cobb/ SuperStock, pp. 10-11; Valentyn Volkov, p. 10 (small); Wendy Farrington, pp. 12-13; Steven D. Collins, p. 12 (left); Visceralimage, p. 12 (middle); Matt Jeppson, p. 12 (right); Age Fotostock/ SuperStock, pp. 14-15; Michael Reynolds/ EPA/ Newscom, p. 15 (small); Carlos E. Santa Maria, pp. 16-17; John Middlebrook/ Cal Sport Media/ Newscom, p. 16 (small); Edwin Remsberg/ Getty Images, p. 18; NASA/ Handout/ Getty Images, p. 19 (small); Visions of America/ SuperStock, pp. 20-21; Maryland Jousting Tournament Association/ Maryland Department of Agriculture, p. 20 (small); Monkey Business Images, p. 22 (small); Yellowj, p. 23; Keller & Keller Photo/ Age Fotostock, p. 23 (small); Mark Wilson/ Getty Images, pp. 24-25; Jerry Pinkney/ National Geographic Image Collection/ Glow Images, pp. 26-27; Dorchester County Tourism, p. 27; Pakmor, p. 28 (top); Mark Herreid, p. 28 (bottom); Nastya Pirieva, p. 29 (left); Al Mueller, p. 29 (right).